Contents

How to Use This Book   2

Skills Correlation Guide   3

Pre-assessment Activities
  Number Sense: Place Value   4
  Whole Number Addition and
    Subtraction: Addition   5
  Whole Number Multiplication
    and Division: Division   6
  Fractions: Multiplying Fractions   7
  Multiples and Factors:
    Least Common Multiples   8
  Decimals: Multiplying Decimals   9

Number Sense
  Teaching Tips   10
  Rounding: Round It Out   11
  Place Value: What's Its Value?   12
  Place Value: Learning About
    Values   13
  Prime Numbers: Prime Time   14
  Post-assessment Activities   15

Whole Number Addition and Subtraction
  Teaching Tips   16
  Addition Problems: Let's
    Practice Adding!   17
  Addition Word Problems:
    Adding with Words   18
  Subtraction Problems: Find
    the Difference   19
  Subtraction Word Problems:
    Planetary Problems   20
  Post-assessment Activities   21

Whole Number Multiplication and Division
  Teaching Tips   22
  Multiplication Problems:
    Let's Multiply!   23

Multiplication Word Problems:
    Multiplication Station   24
  Division Problems:
    Dividing Time   25
  Division Word Problems:
    Real-World Division   26
  Post-assessment Activities   27

Fractions
  Teaching Tips   28
  Lowest Terms: How Low Can
    You Go?   29
  Improper Fractions and Mixed
    Numbers: That's Improper!   30
  Adding and Subtracting Like
    Fractions: Like Fractions   31
  Multiplying Fractions: Fractions,
    Fractions, Fractions   32
  Post-assessment Activities   33

Multiples and Factors
  Teaching Tips   34
  Multiples: Multiple Multiples   35
  Least Common Multiples:
    The Least in Common   36
  Factors: Finding Factors   37
  Greatest Common Factors: The
    Greatest Factors on Earth!   38
  Post-assessment Activities   39

Decimals
  Teaching Tips   40
  Adding and Subtracting Decimals:
    Getting to the Point   41
  Decimal Word Problems:
    Decimals in Our World   42
  Multiplying Decimals:
    Multiplication with Decimals   43
  Dividing Decimals: Decimal
    Division   44
  Post-assessment Activities   45

Answer Key   46

How to Use This Book

Numbers and Operations helps your fifth-grade learner establish a strong foundation in the identification and manipulation of numbers, skills essential to later mathematical studies. *Numbers and Operations* presents stimulating activities, based on standards set by the National Council of Teachers of Mathematics (NCTM), which challenge and engage learners, enabling them to gain confidence in their mathematical abilities.

This Brain Builders activity book features six sections, each highlighting a different aspect of the fifth-grade math curriculum. Each section presents four activities with easy-to-follow directions, skill definitions, and examples. Many of the activities also feature kid-friendly fun facts related to the subject matter, designed to show learners how math exists in the world around them.

Number Sense
The first section of this book focuses on a variety of basic number concepts. Learners gain valuable practice working with place value, rounding, and prime numbers.

Whole Number Addition and Subtraction
The second section of this book concentrates on addition and subtraction. Through basic problems and word problems, learners strengthen their knowledge of these core skills.

Whole Number Multiplication and Division
The third section of this book develops learners' abilities in solving multiplication and division problems. As learners work with basic and word problems, they use both their computational and analytical skills.

Fractions
The fourth section of this book develops learners' abilities to manipulate fractions. The activities challenge learners to reduce fractions to their lowest terms; change improper fractions to mixed numbers; and to add, subtract, and multiply fractions.

Multiples and Factors

The fifth section of this book involves multiples and factors. Learners' multiplication skills are engaged as they find multiples, least common multiples, factors, and greatest common factors.

Decimals

The sixth section of this book concentrates on decimals. The activities require learners to apply their knowledge of decimals in basic addition, subtraction, multiplication, and division problems, as well as in word problems.

Skills Correlation Guide

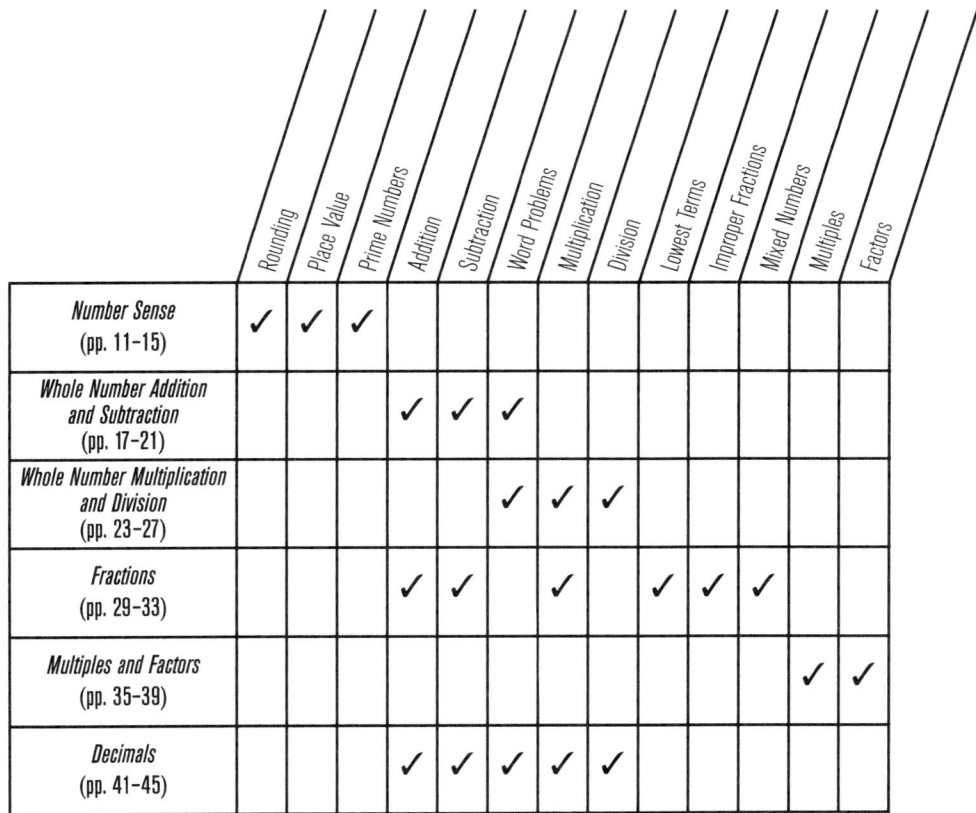

	Rounding	Place Value	Prime Numbers	Addition	Subtraction	Word Problems	Multiplication	Division	Lowest Terms	Improper Fractions	Mixed Numbers	Multiples	Factors
Number Sense (pp. 11-15)	✓	✓	✓										
Whole Number Addition and Subtraction (pp. 17-21)				✓	✓	✓							
Whole Number Multiplication and Division (pp. 23-27)						✓	✓	✓					
Fractions (pp. 29-33)				✓	✓		✓		✓	✓	✓		
Multiples and Factors (pp. 35-39)												✓	✓
Decimals (pp. 41-45)				✓	✓	✓	✓	✓					

The activities featured in this book are level U according to the guidelines set by Fountas and Pinnell.

PRE-ASSESSMENT ACTIVITIES
Number Sense

Name _____

Place Value

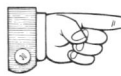 Directions: Find the place value of the digit 3 in each number below. Write your answers on the lines provided.

1. 6,348,012 _____

2. 3,219 _____

3. 436,045 _____

4. 700,329 _____

5. 3,908,455 _____

6. 58,403 _____

 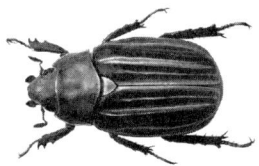 

4

© Rosen School Supply•Brain Builders Numbers and Operations•5•RSS-8576-8

PRE-ASSESSMENT ACTIVITIES
Whole Number Addition and Subtraction

Name _____

Addition

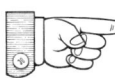 **Directions: Solve each problem below.**

1. 6,029,681
      892,418
  +   430,112

2.   182,309
      926,842
  +   704,040

3.   102,791
      805,033
  +   688,688

4. 1,257,984
      512,000
  +   271,296

5. 3,121,549
      264,888
  +   695,430

6.   744,001
      396,233
  +   120,019

PRE-ASSESSMENT ACTIVITIES

Whole Number Multiplication and Division

Name _____

Division

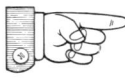 **Directions:** Solve each problem below. Use a separate sheet of paper if you need more space. Write your answers on the lines provided.

1. 783 ÷ 21 = _____   2. 306 ÷ 61 = _____

3. 432 ÷ 20 = _____   4. 6,204 ÷ 42 = _____

5. 735 ÷ 12 = _____   6. 921 ÷ 39 = _____

PRE-ASSESSMENT ACTIVITIES
Fractions

Name _____

Multiplying Fractions

 **Directions:** Solve each problem below. If necessary, reduce your answer to its lowest terms. Write your answers on the lines provided.

1. $\dfrac{6}{7} \times \dfrac{4}{5} =$ _____

2. $\dfrac{3}{7} \times \dfrac{2}{9} =$ _____

3. $\dfrac{6}{8} \times \dfrac{1}{3} =$ _____

4. $\dfrac{1}{2} \times \dfrac{1}{2} =$ _____

5. $\dfrac{6}{9} \times \dfrac{5}{4} =$ _____

6. $\dfrac{7}{8} \times \dfrac{2}{3} =$ _____

PRE-ASSESSMENT ACTIVITIES

Multiples and Factors

Name _____

Least Common Multiples

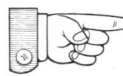 **Directions:** Find the least common multiple of each pair of numbers below. Write your answers on the lines provided.

1. 6 and 8 _____

2. 2 and 5 _____

3. 4 and 6 _____

4. 3 and 2 _____

5. 5 and 4 _____

6. 9 and 3 _____

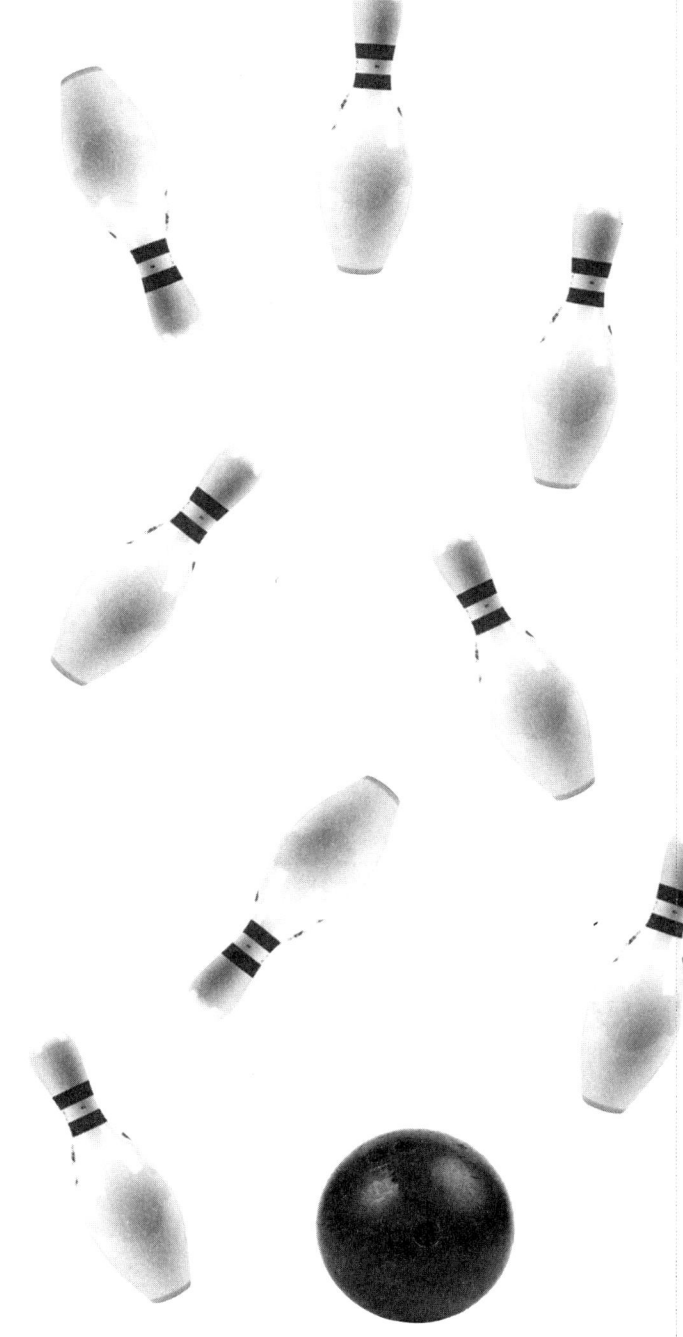

PRE-ASSESSMENT ACTIVITIES

Decimals

Multiplying Decimals

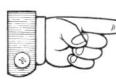 **Directions: Solve each problem below.**

1. 2.3
   × 6.4

2. 6.1
   × 0.4

3. 7.6
   × 1.9

4. 5.1
   × 8.7

5. 6.7
   × 4.2

6. 2.8
   × 9.4

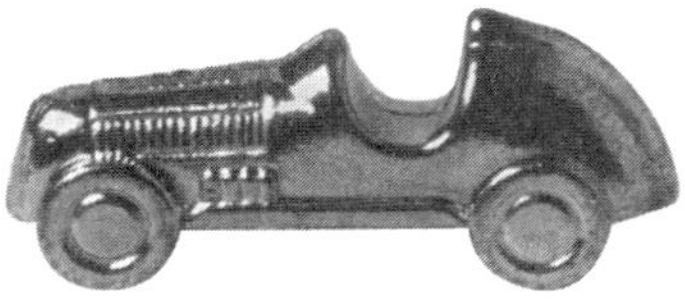

For *Number Sense* (pp. 11–15)

Background
- In this section, learners gain valuable practice working with a variety of number concepts. The activities involve rounding, place value, and prime number comprehension.

Homework Helper
- After completing the activity on page 11, have learners write out the area of each state in word form. This exercise will reinforce learners' comprehension of place value while giving them an opportunity to practice writing numbers in word form.

Research-based Activity
- Have learners create comparison charts, like the one featured in the activity on page 11, showing the area, population, or another statistic for a chosen set of cities. Learners can use the Internet to find the information needed for their charts.

Test Prep
- The activities in this section help learners develop a strong sense of number relationships. This valuable practice will enable learners to succeed on both classroom and standardized tests.

Different Audiences
- Challenge an accelerated learner by having him or her expand on the research-based activity above. After completing the research, have the learner write number sentences comparing the statistics of their chosen cities or countries. To write the number sentences, learners should use the concepts of less than, greater than, and equal to.

Group Activity
- Divide learners into small groups and present each group with a news article that features statistical information. Have learners work together to find any places in the article where numbers have been rounded. Each group should present their findings, explaining the place value to which each number was rounded. This exercise will provide learners with an understanding of how rounded numbers are used outside of the classroom.

NUMBER SENSE
Rounding

Name _____

Round It Out

To round a number is to increase or decrease that number to the nearest 10, 100, 1000, and so on. To round the number 34,706 to the nearest thousand, we first find the digit in the thousands place. That digit is 4. Next, we look at the digit one place to the right of the 4. That digit, 7, is in the hundreds place. Since 7 is greater than 5, we change the 4 in the thousands place to a 5 and change each digit to the right of that digit to a 0. Therefore, 34,706 rounded to the nearest thousand is 35,000.
Example: The number 34,581,392 rounded to the nearest million is 35,000,000.

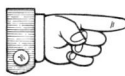 **Directions:** Use the chart to help you fill in the answers below. Write your answers on the lines.

LARGEST STATES IN UNITED STATES OF AMERICA

States	Alaska	Texas	California	Montana	New Mexico	Arizona
Area in Square Miles	656,424	268,581	163,707	147,046	121,598	114,006

1. Round the area of California to the nearest thousand.
   _____

2. Which state's area rounded to the nearest hundred thousand would be 200,000 square miles?
   _____

3. List three states with areas that would be 100,000 square miles when rounded to the nearest hundred thousand.
   _____

4. Round the area of Alaska to the nearest ten thousand.
   _____

NUMBER SENSE
Place Value

Name _____

What's Its Value?

A digit is any one of the ten symbols 0, 1, 2, 3, 4, 5, 6, 7, 8, or 9 that is used to write numbers. Place value is the value of a single digit depending on its place in a number.
Example: In the number 1,602,459, the digit 6 is in the hundred thousands place.

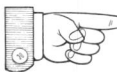 **Directions:** Find the place value of the digit 2 in each number below. Write your answers on the lines provided.

1. 621 _____

2. 7,241,600 _____

3. 2,035,981 _____

4. 1,502,134 _____

5. 720,496 _____

6. 681,204 _____

FUN FACT
The United States and England have different numbering systems. In the United States, 1,000,000,000 is called a billion. In England, the same number is called a milliard.

12

© Rosen School Supply•Brain Builders Numbers and Operations•5•RSS-8576-8

NUMBER SENSE
Place Value

Name _____

Learning About Values

A digit is any one of the ten symbols 0, 1, 2, 3, 4, 5, 6, 7, 8, or 9 that is used to write numbers. Place value is the value of a single digit depending on its place in a number.
Example: In the number 27,645,980, the digit 4 is in the ten thousands place.

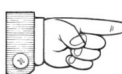 **Directions:** Look at the number below. Then write the correct digit in each place listed.

75,486,092

1. thousands place _____

2. hundred thousands place _____

3. tens place _____

4. ten millions place _____

5. hundreds place _____

6. ones place _____

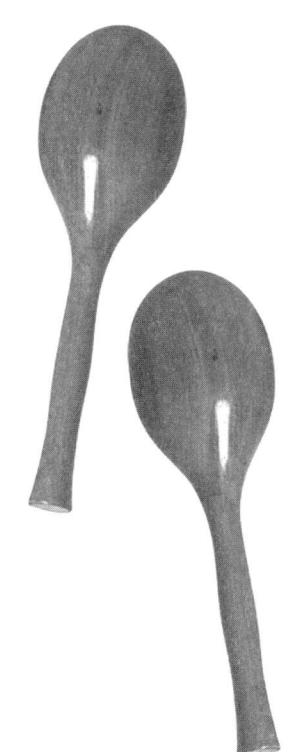

FUN FACT
In the Spanish language, *one thousand* is *un mil.*

13

© Rosen School Supply•Brain Builders Numbers and Operations•5•RSS-8576-8

NUMBER SENSE
Prime Numbers

Name _____

Prime Time

A prime number is a whole number that is greater than 1 and can only be equally divided by 1 and itself.
Example: The number 7 is a prime number. It can only be equally divided by 1 and 7.

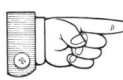 **Directions: Circle each prime number and the letter below it. Cross out all of the other numbers and letters to read the answer to the riddle.**

RIDDLE: Where does Friday come before Thursday?

```
37  51  81  52  67  23  128  71  20  88  59
I   N   S   T   A   D   N    I   F   A   C


43  75  29  99  2   111  5   83  9   19
T   T   I   N   O   G    N   A   T   R


21  30  17
S   W   Y
```

FUN FACT
The number 2 is the only even prime number.

14

© Rosen School Supply•Brain Builders Numbers and Operations•5•RSS-8576-8

POST-ASSESSMENT ACTIVITIES   Name _____

Skill Check—Number Sense

Rounding

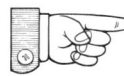 **Directions: Round the number below to the nearest ten thousand.**

682,014 _____

Place Value

 **Directions: Find the place value of the digit 4 in the number below.**

4,023,981 _____

Prime Numbers

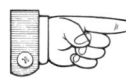 **Directions: Circle each prime number below.**

16   29   35   67   17   32

Teaching Tips...

For *Whole Numbers Addition and Subtraction* (pp. 17–21)

Background
- In this section, learners develop their addition and subtraction skills. The activities feature basic addition and subtraction problems as well as addition and subtraction word problems.

Homework Helper
- Have learners create addition and subtraction word problems using their own lives as inspiration. Once finished, learners can exchange problems with one another to complete as homework assignments.

Research-based Activity
- Have learners research the dates of several major inventions. Ask learners to write subtraction problems to determine how long ago each item was invented. This exercise will help learners practice subtraction while increasing their knowledge of historical events.

Test Prep
- Addition and subtraction are fundamental concepts that learners should master as early as possible. As these concepts are essential to everyday life, they are frequently featured on standardized tests. The activities in this section provide learners with ample practice for success in these areas.

Different Audiences
- Have a learner for whom English is a second language (ESL) research changes in the population of his or her native country over the past few decades. Help the learner create word problems using those numbers. This exercise will encourage mastery of the English language while allowing the learner to deal with a comfortable topic.

Group Activity
- Separate learners into five groups. Assign each group ten of the fifty states that make up the United States of America. Have each group work together to research statistical information about their states. Next, ask groups to write addition and subtraction word problems using the information they have found. Groups can then exchange and solve each others' word problems.

WHOLE NUMBER ADDITION AND SUBTRACTION
Addition Problems

Name _____

Let's Practice Adding!

To add numbers is to join them together to find a sum, or total amount.
Example: 4,563,245
         + 2,197,465
            6,760,710

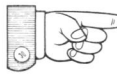 **Directions:** Solve each problem below. Use a separate sheet of paper if you need more space.

1.   2,680,491
       879,703
     + 321,007

2.   2,511,296
     1,792,806
     + 604,293

3.   881,204
     679,312
     + 501,967

4.   3,681,988
        92,605
     +1,365,722

5.   936,411
     149,287
     + 896,302

6.   4,111,111
       202,399
     + 700,004

FUN FACT
The ancient Greeks called the number 10,000 a myriad.

17

WHOLE NUMBER ADDITION AND SUBTRACTION

Addition Word Problems

Name _____

Adding with Words

We can use addition to solve real-world math problems.
Example: Ben has 565 baseball cards. For his birthday, he received 25 more from his parents, 32 more from his grandmother, and 100 more from his uncle. How many cards does Ben have now?
565 + 25 + 32 + 100 = 722. Ben has 722 cards.

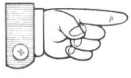 **Directions: Solve the following word problems. Write your answers on the lines provided. Use a separate sheet of paper if you need more space.**

1. The three largest populations in Tennessee are in the cities of Memphis, Nashville, and Knoxville. There are 650,100 people in Memphis, 569,891 people in Nashville, and 173,890 people in Knoxville. What is the total number of people living in these three cities?

   _____

2. In Tennessee, there are 84,640 miles (136,215 kilometers) of road and 2,205 miles (3,549 km) of railroad tracks. What is the combined total number of miles of roads and railroad tracks?

   _____

3. Between 1980 and 1990, the population of Tennessee increased by 286,185 people. Between 1990 and 2000, the population of Tennessee increased by 812,098 people. What is the total increase in population between 1980 and 2000?

   _____

FUN FACT
The state bird of Tennessee is the mockingbird and the state flower is the iris.

18

WHOLE NUMBER ADDITION AND SUBTRACTION

Subtraction Problems

Name _____

Find the Difference

To subtract is to find out how much is left over after taking one number away from another number.

Example: 85,089
         − 20,156
         ─────────
            64,933

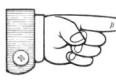 **Directions: Solve each problem below.**

1.   62,421
   − 29,687

2.   39,046
   − 12,651

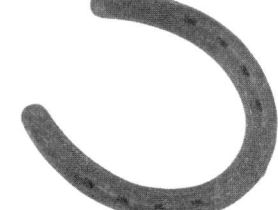

3.   70,591
   − 18,022

4.   82,370
   − 56,296

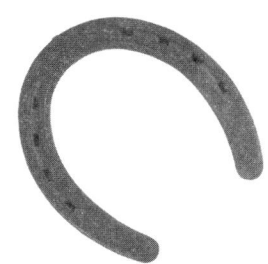

5.   49,207
   − 21,683

6.   90,275
   − 62,402

FUN FACT

If you subtract a bigger number from a smaller number, you get a number less than zero. This is called a negative number.

19

© Rosen School Supply•Brain Builders Numbers and Operations•5•RSS-8576-8

WHOLE NUMBER ADDITION AND SUBTRACTION
Subtraction Word Problems

Name _____

Planetary Problems

We can use subtraction to solve real-world math problems.

Example: The telescope was invented in 1608. Man first walked on the moon in 1969. How many years after the telescope was invented did man first walk on the moon?

$$1969 - 1608 = 361 \text{ years}$$

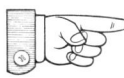 **Directions: Solve the following word problems. Write your answers on the lines provided. Use a separate sheet of paper if you need more space.**

1. The magnifying glass was invented in 1250. The telescope was invented in 1608. How many years later was the telescope invented?

   _____

2. Pluto is 1,458 miles (2,346 kilometers) in diameter. Jupiter is 88,846 miles (142,984 km) in diameter. What is the difference in miles between the diameters of Jupiter and Pluto?

   _____

3. Europa, one of Jupiter's moons, is 416,629 miles (670,499 km) from Jupiter. Metis, another one of Jupiter's moons, is 79,469 miles (127,893 km) from Jupiter. How many miles closer to Jupiter is Metis than Europa?

   _____

FUN FACT
Pluto was first discovered in 1930 by Clyde Tombaugh.

© Rosen School Supply•Brain Builders Numbers and Operations•5•RSS-8576-8

POST-ASSESSMENT ACTIVITIES   Name _____

Skill Check—Whole Number Addition and Subtraction

Addition Problems

 **Directions: Solve each problem below.**

1. 2,956,002
    1,203,683
    + 842,763

2. 3,456,972
    1,902,008
    + 8,000,201

3. 9,753,204
    897,100
    + 116,448

Subtraction Word Problems

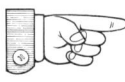 **Directions: Solve the problem below.**

The two smallest countries in the world are Tuvalu, a set of small islands near Australia, and Vatican City, in Rome. There are 11,146 people in Tuvalu and only 860 people in Vatican City. How many more people live in Tuvalu than in Vatican City?

_____

© Rosen School Supply•Brain Builders Numbers and Operations•5•RSS-8576-8

Teaching Tips...

For *Whole Number Multiplication and Division* (pp. 23–27)

Background
- This section encourages learners to build upon basic multiplication and division skills. Learners multiply and divide with two-, three-, and four-digit numbers in both standard problems and word problems.

Homework Helper
- Have learners keep a journal of how many times a week they eat their favorite food or participate in an activity that they enjoy. Based on those numbers, have learners use their knowledge of multiplication to figure out how many times a month and how many times a year they eat that food or participate in that activity.

Research-based Activity
- Have learners use the Internet to research and plan a family vacation. Have each learner choose a location and find out how much the trip might cost. Encourage learners to incorporate airfare, hotel costs, entertainment, car rental, etc. Once they find a total number, have learners divide that number by the number of people in their families to find the cost per person.

Test Prep
- Mastering multiplication and division of large numbers is essential for learners' progression in mathematics. Practice in this area will help learners succeed on classroom tests and in later studies.

Different Audiences
- Help a challenged learner understand the multiplication of large numbers by breaking each multiplicand (the second number in the multiplication problem) down by place value. For example, show the learner that 123 x 419 is equal to the following: (123 x 9) + (123 x 10) + (123 x 400).

Group Activity
- Have a large group of learners act out a series of division problems. Call out various numbers and have learners divide themselves by that number. For example, if the number five was called, learners would separate themselves into five groups. Learners often benefit from a visual display of mathematical concepts.

© Rosen School Supply•Brain Builders Numbers and Operations•5•RSS-8576-8

WHOLE NUMBER MULTIPLICATION AND DIVISION
Division Problems

Name _____

Dividing Time

Division is a process in which a number is broken into a certain number of equal parts. Sometimes, a number cannot be divided equally into another number. The amount that is left over is called the remainder.
Example: 900 ÷ 42 = 21 with a remainder of 18

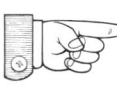 **Directions: Solve each problem below. Write your answers on the lines provided. Use a separate sheet of paper if you need more space.**

1. 697 ÷ 21 = _____ with a remainder of _____

2. 704 ÷ 17 = _____ with a remainder of _____

3. 3,121 ÷ 26 = _____ with a remainder of _____

4. 8,982 ÷ 83 = _____ with a remainder of _____

5. 1,217 ÷ 56 = _____ with a remainder of _____

FUN FACT
Division problems can be written differently. For example, 30 divided by 10 can be written as 30÷10 or $\frac{30}{10}$.

25

Name _____

Real-World Division

We can use division to solve real-world math problems.

Example: Sheila collected $165 in donations for a charity. If she collected money from 15 people and each person gave the same amount, how much money did each person give?

$$165 \div 15 = \$11$$

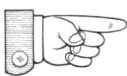 **Directions: Solve the following word problems on a separate sheet of paper. Write your answers on the lines provided.**

1. Diane wants to read 140 pages in 7 days. If she plans to reads an equal number of pages each day, how many pages should she read each day to reach her goal?

   _____

2. Selby has 36 photographs from her vacation. If her photo album has 18 pages, how many photographs can she put on each page?

   _____

3. There are 10 boys and 14 girls in Ms. Garnett's science class. Ms. Garnett breaks the students into 4 equal groups. How many students are in each group?

   _____

4. Mike wants to earn $120. If he makes $5 an hour, how many hours must Mike work to earn $120?

   _____

FUN FACT
You cannot divide a number by zero.

POST-ASSESSMENT ACTIVITIES   Name _____

Skill Check—Whole Number Multiplication and Division

Multiplication Problems

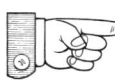 **Directions: Solve each problem below.**

1. 681
    x 425

2. 345
    x 101

3. 772
    x 353

Division Word Problems

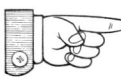 **Directions: Solve the problem below.**

1A. There are 31 students in Ms. Bell's class. She wants to divide them into 5 groups. Can she divide them evenly?

_____

B. If not, how many students will be left over?

_____

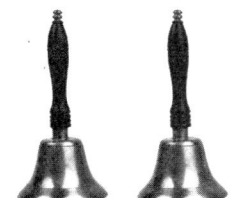
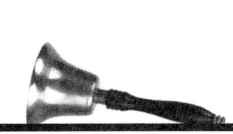

27

For *Fractions* (pp. 29–33)

Background
- In this section, learners gain experience working with fractions. The activities involve reducing fractions to lowest terms, changing improper fractions into mixed numbers, and using fractions to add, subtract, and multiply.

Homework Helper
- Provide learners with a set number of dried beans in various colors. Have learners write the fractions that represent the relationship between each color bean and the total number of beans. Next, have learners add and subtract those fractions from the total number.

Research-based Activity
- Have learners use a dictionary to create a fraction vocabulary list. Key terms, such as *numerator*, *denominator*, and *improper fraction*, should be included.

Test Prep
- In this section, learners hone their fraction skills. The activities provide valuable practice with fraction concepts that are frequently tested in the math classroom at this level.

Different Audiences
- Help a challenged learner master the concept of improper fractions by helping him or her draw diagrams of them. This exercise will teach learners to visualize concepts they might not otherwise understand.

Group Activity
- Hold a fraction bee. Separate learners into groups of two or three and have each group take turns reducing various fractions to their lowest terms. The team with the most correct answers wins the game.

FRACTIONS
Lowest Terms

Name _____

How Low Can You Go?

To reduce a fraction to its lowest terms, we divide the numerator and the denominator by their greatest common factor. The greatest common factor is the largest number that divides evenly into the numerator and denominator.
Example: To reduce $\frac{4}{12}$ to its lowest terms, we find the greatest common factor of 4 and 12. That number is 4.
$4 \div 4 = 1$ $12 \div 4 = 3$ $\frac{4}{12}$ reduced to its lowest terms is $\frac{1}{3}$.

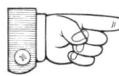 **Directions:** Reduce each fraction below to its lowest terms. Write your answers on the lines provided.

1. $\frac{5}{25}$ _____

2. $\frac{9}{81}$ _____

3. $\frac{6}{21}$ _____

4. $\frac{12}{32}$ _____

5. $\frac{27}{33}$ _____

6. $\frac{8}{64}$ _____

7. $\frac{10}{45}$ _____

8. $\frac{12}{36}$ _____

FUN FACT
Reducing a fraction to its lowest terms is also called simplifying a fraction.

FRACTIONS

Name _____

Improper Fractions and Mixed Numbers

That's Improper!

An improper fraction is a fraction in which the numerator is larger than the denominator. A mixed number is a whole number followed by a fraction. To change an improper fraction into a mixed number, we divide the numerator by the denominator. If the denominator does not divide evenly into the numerator, we place the remainder over the original denominator to make a fraction.
Example: To change $\frac{17}{4}$ into a mixed number, we divide 17 by 4.
$17 \div 4 = 4$ with a remainder of 1. $\frac{17}{4}$ written as a mixed number is $4\frac{1}{4}$.

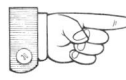 **Directions:** Change each improper fraction below into a mixed number. Write your answers on the lines provided.

1. $\frac{93}{8}$ _____   2. $\frac{8}{7}$ _____

3. $\frac{9}{5}$ _____   4. $\frac{4}{3}$ _____

5. $\frac{11}{9}$ _____   6. $\frac{25}{3}$ _____

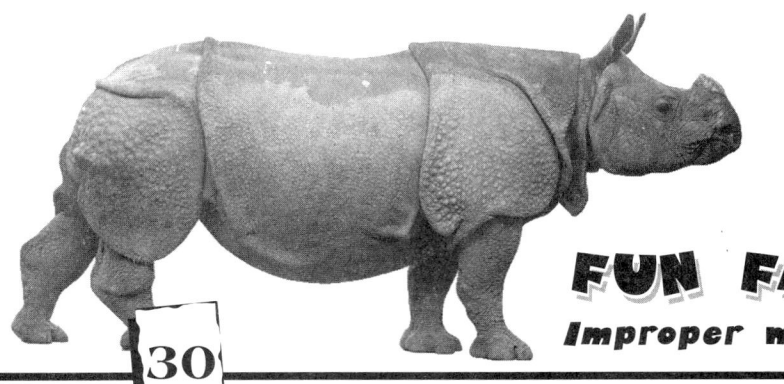

FUN FACT
Improper means not right or not correct.

30

FRACTIONS

Name _____

Adding and Subtracting
Like Fractions

Like Fractions

To add or subtract fractions with like denominators, we add or subtract the numerators. The denominator stays the same.

Example: $\frac{9}{8} - \frac{4}{8} = \frac{5}{8}$

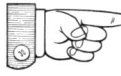 **Directions:** Solve each problem below. Write your answers on the lines provided.

1. $\frac{2}{9} + \frac{6}{9} =$ _____

2. $\frac{4}{5} - \frac{3}{5} =$ _____

3. $\frac{9}{26} + \frac{10}{26} =$ _____

4. $\frac{18}{32} - \frac{11}{32} =$ _____

5. $\frac{3}{16} + \frac{12}{16} =$ _____

6. $\frac{13}{19} - \frac{4}{19} =$ _____

7. $\frac{3}{8} + \frac{2}{8} =$ _____

8. $\frac{14}{20} - \frac{11}{20} =$ _____

FUN FACT
The horizontal fraction bar was first used around the year 1200 A.D. by Arab peoples.

Fractions, Fractions, Fractions

To multiply fractions, we multiply the numerator of the first fraction by the numerator of the second fraction to find the numerator in the answer. Next, we multiply the denominator of the first fraction by the denominator of the second fraction to find the denominator in the answer.

Example: To multiply $\frac{2}{5}$ by $\frac{3}{7}$, we multiply as follows:

$2 \times 3 = 6$
$5 \times 7 = 35$
$\frac{2}{5} \times \frac{3}{7} = \frac{6}{35}$

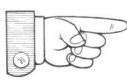 **Directions:** Solve each problem below. Write your answers on the lines provided. If necessary, reduce your answer to its lowest terms.

1. $\frac{7}{11} \times \frac{3}{5} =$ _____

2. $\frac{2}{9} \times \frac{1}{3} =$ _____

3. $\frac{3}{10} \times \frac{2}{5} =$ _____

4. $\frac{2}{9} \times \frac{4}{7} =$ _____

5. $\frac{4}{7} \times \frac{2}{3} =$ _____

6. $\frac{9}{10} \times \frac{7}{8} =$ _____

FUN FACT

When we multiply fractions, we are actually finding a smaller part of the whole number. For example, $\frac{1}{2} \times \frac{1}{2} = \frac{1}{4}$ ($\frac{1}{4} < \frac{1}{2}$)

POST-ASSESSMENT ACTIVITIES   Name _____

Skill Check—Fractions

Reducing Fractions to Lowest Terms

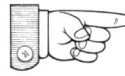 **Directions: Reduce each fraction below to its lowest terms.**

1. $\frac{4}{16}$ _____   2. $\frac{10}{25}$ _____

Improper Fractions and Mixed Numbers

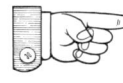 **Directions: Change the improper fraction below into a mixed number.**

1. $\frac{83}{9}$ _____   2. $\frac{57}{8}$ _____

Adding and Subtracting Like Fractions

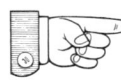 **Directions: Solve each problem below.**

1. $\frac{6}{11} - \frac{2}{11} =$ _____   2. $\frac{8}{17} + \frac{2}{17} =$ _____

**For *Multiples and Factors*
(pp. 35–39)**

Background
- In this section, learners work with multiples and factors. The activities build upon learners' understanding of multiplication and division as they determine greatest common factors and least common multiples.

Homework Helper
- Have learners create a multiplication table using numbers greater than 10. Next, have learners refer to the table to answer questions about multiples and factors of the included numbers. Creating the table will reinforce multiplication skills and give learners a visual reference to use in determining multiples and factors.

Research-based Activity
- Have learners use the Internet to find and print out Pascal's triangle, a triangle of numbers in which each new number in a line is the sum of the two numbers above it. Next, have each learner select a number between two and ten and color each number in the triangle that is a multiple of that number. Finished triangles can be displayed for fun.

Test Prep
- Multiples and factors are important concepts for learners to master at this level and are frequently featured in classroom testing. The activities in this section provide learners with valuable practice for strengthening their abilities in these areas.

Different Audiences
- Challenge advanced learners by presenting them clues with which they can identify numbers. For example, ask a learner to find a number that is a multiple of 2 and a factor of both 20 and 32.

Group Activity
- Divide learners into small groups. Have them make flash cards featuring two numbers on one side and either their greatest common factor or least common multiple on the other side. Next, have learners take turns quizzing each other with the cards to increase their knowledge of multiples and factors.

MULTIPLES AND FACTORS
Multiples

Name _____

Multiple Multiples

A multiple is the product of a number multiplied by any other number.
Example: The first five multiples of 2 are 2, 4, 6, 8, and 10. We find them by multiplying 2 by 1, 2, 3, 4, and 5.

 **Directions: Write the first 5 multiples of each number below.**

1. 3 ____, ____, ____, ____, ____

2. 7 ____, ____, ____, ____, ____

3. 10 ____, ____, ____, ____, ____

4. 9 ____, ____, ____, ____, ____

5. 4 ____, ____, ____, ____, ____

6. 5 ____, ____, ____, ____, ____

FUN FACT
There are an unlimited number of multiples of any number.

35

MULTIPLES AND FACTORS
Least Common Multiples

Name _____

The Least in Common

A multiple is the product of a number multiplied by any other number. The least common multiple of two numbers is the smallest number greater than 0 that is a multiple of both numbers.

Example: The least common multiple of 4 and 6 is 12. 12 is the smallest number that is a multiple of both 4 and 6.

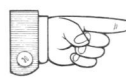 **Directions: Find the least common multiple of each pair of numbers below. Write your answers on the lines provided.**

1. 5 and 3 _____

2. 6 and 2 _____

3. 4 and 10 _____

4. 8 and 10 _____

5. 9 and 6 _____

FUN FACT
Least common multiple is often shortened to LCM.

36

© Rosen School Supply•Brain Builders Numbers and Operations•5•RSS-8576-8

MULTIPLES AND FACTORS

Factors

Name _____

Finding Factors

A factor of a number will divide into that number evenly without any remainder.
Example: The factors of 16 are 1, 2, 4, 8, and 16.

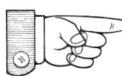 **Directions: Find the factors of each number below. Write your answers on the lines provided.**

1. 10 _____

2. 21 _____

3. 18 _____

4. 32 _____

5. 48 _____

6. 15 _____

FUN FACT

If a number is divisible by 3 and 2, it is also divisible by 6.

MULTIPLES AND FACTORS

Greatest Common Factors

Name _____

The Greatest Factors on Earth!

The greatest common factor of a set of numbers is the largest number that can be divided evenly into both numbers in the set.
Example: The factors of 8 are 1, 2, 4, and 8.
   The factors of 12 are 1, 2, 3, 4, 6, and 12.
   The greatest common factor of 8 and 12 is 4.

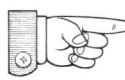 **Directions:** Find the greatest common factor of each pair of numbers. Write your answers on the lines provided.

1. 18 and 30 _____

2. 14 and 35 _____

3. 10 and 25 _____

4. 32 and 20 _____

5. 9 and 33 _____

6. 20 and 46 _____

7. 16 and 56 _____

8. 12 and 39 _____

9. 8 and 52 _____

10. 10 and 34 _____

FUN FACT

Greatest common factor is often shortened to GCF.

POST-ASSESSMENT ACTIVITIES   Name _____

Skill Check—Multiples and Factors

Multiples

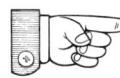 **Directions: Write the first 5 multiples of each number below.**

1. 8 _____, _____, _____, _____, _____

2. 11 _____, _____, _____, _____, _____

Least Common Multiples

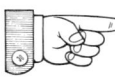 **Directions: Find the least common multiple of each pair of numbers below.**

1. 8 and 3 _____   2. 2 and 9 _____

3. 5 and 10 _____   4. 6 and 7 _____

Greatest Common Factors

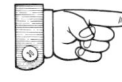 **Directions: Find the greatest common factor of each pair of numbers below.**

1. 16 and 18 _____   2. 36 and 9 _____

3. 4 and 24 _____   4. 12 and 27 _____

39

© Rosen School Supply•Brain Builders Numbers and Operations•5•RSS-8576-8

For *Decimals* (pp. 41–45)

Background
- In this section, learners build their comprehension of decimals. The following activities provide learners with valuable practice in adding, subtracting, multiplying, and dividing decimals through both basic and word problems.

Homework Helper
- Provide learners with menus from local restaurants and have them figure out how much it would cost to go out to dinner with their families. Learners should figure out the total bill to practice their addition skills as well as divide the total by the number of people in their families to practice dividing with decimals.

Research-based Activity
- For a lesson in real-world math, have learners use the Internet to research the minimum wage in the United States. Next, have learners compute how much a worker earning minimum wage would earn in a week, a month, a year, and so on.

Test Prep
- In this section, learners build a strong foundation in working with decimals. The following activities engage learners while preparing them for classroom testing in this area.

Different Audiences
- Help a learner for whom English is a second language (ESL) practice his or her English-language skills by having the learner write out the answers to the word problems in this section in word form. This exercise will also reinforce the learner's understanding of place values.

Group Activity
- Divide learners into several groups. Give each group a pile of coins. Have learners add the coins together to find the total amount of money they have and divide that total by the number of people in the group to find out how much money each would get if they divided the money evenly.

© Rosen School Supply•Brain Builders Numbers and Operations•5•RSS-8576-8

DECIMALS

Adding and Subtracting Decimals

Name _____

Getting to the Point

A decimal is a number with one or more digits to the right of the decimal point. The numbers to the left of the decimal point are whole numbers. The numbers to the right of the point are fractions. The first number to the right of the decimal point is in the tenths place and the second number is in the hundredths place. To add or subtract decimals, we line up the decimal points.

Examples:

```
    30.42            45.26
  + 86.21          − 24.23
   _____           _____
   116.63            21.03
```

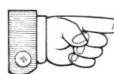 **Directions: Solve each problem below. Use a separate sheet of paper if you need more space.**

1.   4.65
   + 0.46

2.   17.82
   + 48.31

3. 156.38
   − 47.22

4.   87.51
   − 29.38

5. 243.33
   + 62.81

6.   92.28
   − 24.19

FUN FACT

The decimal point was first used in 1616.

41

© Rosen School Supply•Brain Builders Numbers and Operations•5•RSS-8576-8

DECIMALS

Decimal Word Problems

Name _____

Decimals in Our World

To add or subtract decimals, we line up the decimal points.

Examples: 10.59   234.54
           − .54   + 16.42
           ‾‾‾‾‾   ‾‾‾‾‾‾‾
             10.05   250.96

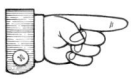 **Directions:** Solve the following word problems. Write the addition or subtraction problem for each by lining up the decimal points. Use a separate sheet of paper if you need more space.

1. Kelly has $50. She buys a shirt for $25.99 and a pair of earrings for $10.50. If the sales tax is $1.82, how much money does Kelly have left?

    _____

2. Jason bought a sandwich for $5.75, apple juice for $.89, a banana for $.25, and a bag of chips for $.99. How much did Jason spend on lunch?

    _____

3. Hakuri's mom gave him $25 to buy groceries. He bought salmon for $6.72, rice for $1.99, tomatoes for $2.39, and onions for $1.89. How much money did Hakuri have left over after buying groceries?

    _____

4. Sadie took her friend Jane out to dinner at a restaurant. She spent $3.50 on drinks, $12.98 on Jane's dinner, and $10.95 on her own dinner. If the tax was $1.37, how much did Sadie spend in total?

    _____

© Rosen School Supply • Brain Builders Numbers and Operations • 5 • RSS-8576-8

DECIMALS

Multiplying Decimals

Multiplication with Decimals

To multiply decimal numbers, we line up the numbers on the right. Then, starting at the right, we multiply each digit in the top number by each digit in the bottom number. Next, we add the products together. Finally, we add the number of decimal places in the top number to the number of decimal places in the bottom number to find the number of decimal places in our answer.

Example: 7.5 x 3.1 = ?

```
      7.5     (1 decimal place)
    x 3.1     (1 decimal place)
    -----
       75
    + 225
    -----
    23.25     (2 decimal places)
```

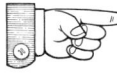 **Directions:** Use the space provided to solve each problem below. Write your answers on the lines provided. Use a separate sheet of paper if you need more space.

1. 9.5 x 0.3 = _____

2. 4.2 x 1.1 = _____

3. .01 x .18 = _____

4. 6.1 x 2.02 = _____

5. 3.2 x 0.4 = _____

6. 8.1 x 3.8 = _____

DECIMALS
Dividing Decimals

Name _____

Decimal Division

In a division problem, the dividend is the number being divided. When dividing a decimal, we line up the decimal point in the answer with the decimal point in the dividend.

Example:
```
       28.2
    2 ⟌ 56.4
       4
       ―
       16
       16
       ――
        04
         4
         ―
         0
```

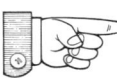 **Directions:** Solve each problem below. Use a separate sheet of paper if you need more space.

1. 4 ⟌ 69.4   2. 2 ⟌ 401.6   3. 3 ⟌ 112.5

4. 9 ⟌ 36.18   5. 2 ⟌ 123.8   6. 3 ⟌ 223.2

FUN FACT
To figure out whether or not a number can be divided evenly by 3, add the digits of that number together. If the digits add up to a multiple of three, the number is evenly divisible by three.

44

© Rosen School Supply•Brain Builders Numbers and Operations•5•RSS-8576-8

POST-ASSESSMENT ACTIVITIES Name _____

Skill Check—Decimals

Adding and Subtracting Decimals

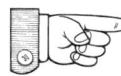 **Directions: Solve each problem below.**

1. 608.24   2. 798.31   3. 843.26
  + 33.61   − 24.09   + 51.19

Multiplying Decimals

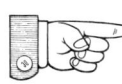 **Directions: Solve each problem below.**

1. 6.2 x 1.9 = _____   2. 3.4 x 2.6 = _____

Dividing Decimals

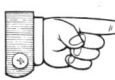 **Directions: Solve each problem below.**

1. 4 ⟌ 169.2   2. 2 ⟌ 35.2

© Rosen School Supply • Brain Builders Numbers and Operations • 5 • RSS-8576-8

Answer Key

p. 4
1. hundred thousands
2. thousands
3. ten thousands
4. hundreds
5. millions
6. ones

p. 5
1. 7,352,211
2. 1,813,191
3. 1,596,512
4. 2,041,280
5. 4,081,867
6. 1,260,253

p. 6
1. 37 with a remainder of 6
2. 5 with a remainder of 1
3. 21 with a remainder of 12
4. 147 with a remainder of 30
5. 61 with a remainder of 3
6. 23 with a remainder of 24

p. 7
1. $\frac{24}{35}$
2. $\frac{2}{21}$
3. $\frac{1}{4}$
4. $\frac{1}{4}$
5. $\frac{5}{6}$
6. $\frac{7}{12}$

p. 8
1. 24
2. 10
3. 12
4. 6
5. 20
6. 9

p. 9
1. 14.72
2. 2.44
3. 14.44
4. 44.37
5. 28.14
6. 26.32

p. 11
1. 164,000 square miles
2. California
3. Montana, New Mexico, Arizona
4. 660,000 square miles

p. 12
1. tens
2. hundred thousands
3. millions
4. thousands
5. ten thousands
6. hundreds

p. 13
1. 6
2. 4
3. 9
4. 7
5. 0
6. 2

p. 14
37 51 67
I   N   A
23 71 59 43 29 2 5 83 19 17
D I C T I O N A R Y

p. 15
Rounding
680,000

Place Value
millions

Prime Numbers
29, 67, and 17 should be circled.

p. 17
1. 3,881,201
2. 4,908,395
3. 2,062,483
4. 5,140,315
5. 1,982,000
6. 5,013,514

p. 18
1. 1,393,881
2. 86,845
3. 1,098,283

p. 19
1. 32,734
2. 26,395
3. 52,569
4. 26,074
5. 27,524
6. 27,873

46

© Rosen School Supply•Brain Builders Numbers and Operations•5•RSS-8576-8

p. 20
1. 358
2. 87,388
3. 337,160

p. 21
Addition Problems
1. 5,002,448
2. 13,359,181
3. 10,766,752

Subtraction Word Problems
10,286

p. 23
1. 100,750
2. 529,322
3. 111,156
4. 190,631
5. 131,868
6. 199,926

p. 24
1. 2,322
2. 43,906
3. 1,460,000

p. 25
1. 33 with a remainder of 4
2. 41 with a remainder of 7
3. 120 with a remainder of 1
4. 108 with a remainder of 18
5. 21 with a remainder of 41

p. 26
1. 20
2. 2
3. 6
4. 24

p. 27
Multiplication Problems
1. 289,425
2. 34,845
3. 272,516

Division Word Problems
1A. no
 B. 1

p. 29
1. $\frac{1}{5}$
2. $\frac{1}{9}$
3. $\frac{2}{7}$
4. $\frac{3}{8}$
5. $\frac{9}{11}$
6. $\frac{1}{8}$
7. $\frac{2}{9}$
8. $\frac{1}{3}$

p. 30
1. $11\frac{5}{8}$
2. $1\frac{1}{7}$
3. $1\frac{4}{5}$
4. $1\frac{1}{3}$
5. $1\frac{2}{9}$
6. $8\frac{1}{3}$

p. 31
1. $\frac{8}{9}$
2. $\frac{1}{5}$
3. $\frac{19}{26}$
4. $\frac{7}{32}$
5. $\frac{15}{16}$
6. $\frac{9}{19}$
7. $\frac{5}{8}$
8. $\frac{3}{20}$

p. 32
1. $\frac{21}{55}$
2. $\frac{2}{27}$
3. $\frac{3}{25}$
4. $\frac{8}{63}$
5. $\frac{8}{21}$
6. $\frac{63}{80}$

p. 33
Reducing Fractions to Lowest Terms
1. $\frac{1}{4}$
2. $\frac{2}{5}$

Improper Fractions and Mixed Numbers
1. $9\frac{2}{9}$
2. $7\frac{1}{8}$

Adding and Subtracting Like Fractions
1. $\frac{4}{11}$
2. $\frac{10}{17}$

p. 35
1. 3, 6, 9, 12, 15
2. 7, 14, 21, 28, 35
3. 10, 20, 30, 40, 50
4. 9, 18, 27, 36, 45
5. 4, 8, 12, 16, 20
6. 5, 10, 15, 20, 25

p. 36
1. 15
2. 6
3. 20

4. 40
5. 18

p. 37
1. 1, 2, 5, 10
2. 1, 3, 7, 21
3. 1, 2, 3, 6, 9, 18
4. 1, 2, 4, 8, 16, 32
5. 1, 2, 3, 4, 6, 8, 12, 16, 24, 48
6. 1, 3, 5, 15

p. 38
1. 6
2. 7
3. 5
4. 4
5. 3
6. 2
7. 8
8. 3
9. 4
10. 2

p. 39
Multiples
1. 8, 16, 24, 32, 40
2. 11, 22, 33, 44, 55

Least Common Multiples
1. 24
2. 18
3. 10
4. 42

Greatest Common Factors
1. 2
2. 9
3. 4
4. 3

p. 41
1. 5.11
2. 66.13
3. 109.16
4. 58.13
5. 306.14
6. 68.09

p. 42
1. $11.69
2. $7.88
3. $12.01
4. $28.80

p. 43
1. 2.85
2. 4.62
3. .0018
4. 12.322
5. 1.28
6. 30.78

p. 44
1. 17.35
2. 200.8
3. 37.5
4. 4.02
5. 61.9
6. 74.4

p. 45
Adding and Subtracting Decimals
1. 641.85
2. 774.22
3. 894.45

Multiplying Decimals
1. 11.78
2. 8.84

Dividing Decimals
1. 42.3
2. 17.6